Mister Descartes and his Evil Genius

Mister Descartes
and his Evil Genius

Narrated by
Jean Paul Mongin

Illustrated by
François Schwoebel

Translated by
Anna Street

Plato & Co.
diaphanes

It was a peaceful night in the winter of 1629 in Holland.
Sitting in the warmth of his stove as it hummed and smoked,
Mister Descartes, gentleman, soldier and traveler,
was at his writing table.

While the entire town, including his parrot Baruch,
had been asleep for a long time already, Mister Descartes,
deciphering the great book of the world, was studying the
optimal size of lenses and meteors.

Now that the snow had stopped falling, the glare of the moon
threw a fearsome silhouette of Baruch the parrot into the room.
In the blink of an eyelid, Mister Descartes thought
he could detect something lurking in the shadow of his pet…
an Evil Genius who engineered illusions!

For Mister Descartes, his room, Holland and the world appeared
in all their strangeness, and perhaps as mere tricks of the mind
of the Evil Genius. Baruch, the faithful bird, and the body of
Mister Descartes, could they be nothing but creatures of his
imagination?

Mister Descartes was beset by doubts:

*Have I not since my childhood taken a host of
false opinions to be true, like when I believed
that the sun revolved around the earth?*

Have I not sometimes felt that my senses
were deceiving me? Did I not even base myself
on this deception to invent some feints
in my treatise on fencing?

But can I reasonably doubt that I am really here,
in my room close to the fire? And how could I doubt
that these hands and this body belong to me?

Or am I like the insane who affirm constantly that they are kings, though they are very poor, and that they are clothed in gold and royal purple, though they are completely bare, or that imagine themselves to be jugs or to have a body made of glass?

"Insane! Insane!" croaked Baruch.

Or was Mister Descartes in the middle of a dream?
Was he thinking he was dreaming or dreaming
he was thinking of dreaming?

If the sky, the earth, colors, faces, sounds,
if my hands, my eyes, my senses are but parts of a dream,
of what can I be truly certain?

Or perhaps the Evil Genius makes me feel aware even of time, space and numbers while, really, there are no such things. Maybe three plus two does not equal five, and the Evil Genius causes me to be mistaken every time I count?

Mister Descartes decided that, in order to arrive at any certainty, he would have to watch out for the Evil Genius' crafty tricks. He would stop taking anything for granted, and act as though nothing and no one truly existed. Baruch gave him a funny look. Mister Descartes would clearly have to solve the problem on his own.

This brought to mind Mister Descartes' friend Anatole Archimède, who claimed that in order to shift the earth's globe and transport it to another location, all that was needed was one fixed and secure point.

In the same way, I must find one thing that is sure and beyond doubt.

For one thing remains certain:
admittedly, the Evil Genius, disguised as Baruch,
strove hard to deceive Mister Descartes constantly
and to fill his mind with illusions; but Mister Descartes
himself, the victim of these clever tricks, had to exist,
since he thought of all this!

Eureka!!! I think, I am, this is what cannot be doubted!

Full of enthusiasm, he picked up his favorite quill.
The Evil Genius might have tricked him into thinking
that he had a body, that he lived in a world,
that three plus two equaled five… In spite of all that,
Mister Descartes could affirm with absolute certainty:

I am a thinking thing!

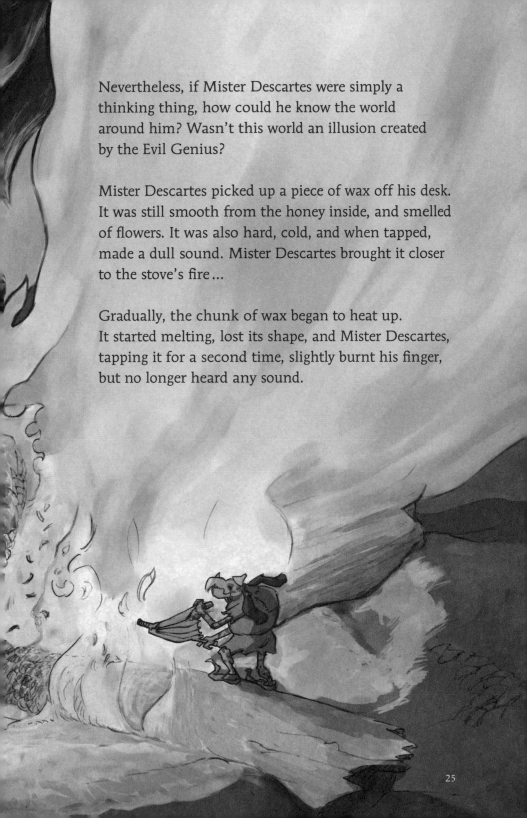

Nevertheless, if Mister Descartes were simply a
thinking thing, how could he know the world
around him? Wasn't this world an illusion created
by the Evil Genius?

Mister Descartes picked up a piece of wax off his desk.
It was still smooth from the honey inside, and smelled
of flowers. It was also hard, cold, and when tapped,
made a dull sound. Mister Descartes brought it closer
to the stove's fire...

Gradually, the chunk of wax began to heat up.
It started melting, lost its shape, and Mister Descartes,
tapping it for a second time, slightly burnt his finger,
but no longer heard any sound.

Nonetheless, it is indeed the very same piece of wax...
Yet it is no longer smooth like honey, nor does it smell of flowers,
nor does it have the same shape, nor make the same sound...
I reckon that is it the exact same wax, but my senses tell me
otherwise... How can I recognize this wax that appears so
different to me now?

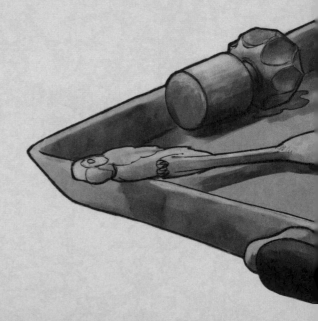

The shouts of a few late passers-by coming out of a tavern drew Mister Descartes to his window.

And these hats and these coats that I see going by in the street, which I believe to be people—how do I know they are not ghosts in disguise? And what if under his feathers, Baruch was just a robot triggered by springs? How do all these things on the outside of me prove anything other than the existence of my own self, Mister Descartes, who is watching or imagining them?

In the end, Mister Descartes, unable to know anything apart from his own mind, decided to put himself to bed, and blew out his candle.

Now I will close my eyes, I will plug my ears, I will shut down all my senses, I will erase all the images from my mind. By meditation, I will attempt to render myself better known and more familiar to myself.

"You yourself!" hissed Baruch who wanted to sleep.

Mister Descartes, snuggled tightly into his nightcap, delved deep into his mind, and began searching for things which are quite certain and obvious.

Many ideas went through his mind:
the earth, the sky, the stars, his first, slightly
cross-eyed girlfriend, the chunk of wax,
and all the things he had once encountered.
But the task was to make sure that these ideas
corresponded to real things...

For example, I have in my mind the idea of the sun that I saw shining yesterday, extremely small in the sky; and another idea of the sun that astronomy gives me, according to which the sun appears several times bigger than the earth. These two ideas cannot refer to the same sun!

But of course, the ideas about the sun come to me
from somewhere. There is at least as much reality in
the cause of these ideas as in the ideas themselves...

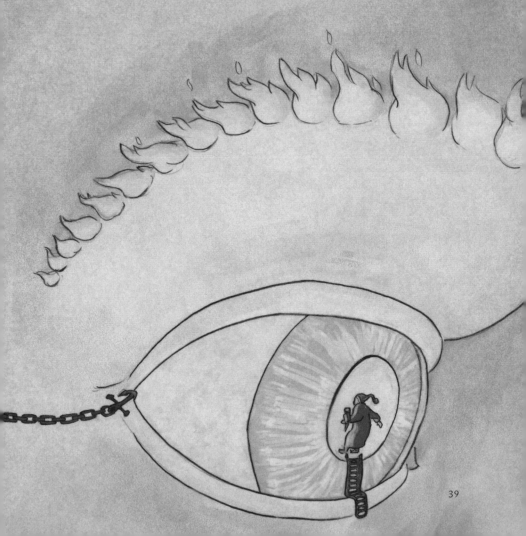

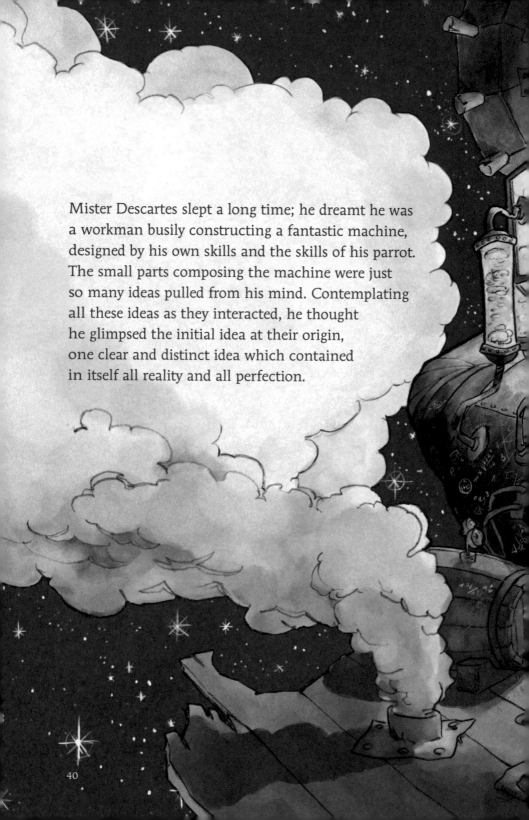

Mister Descartes slept a long time; he dreamt he was
a workman busily constructing a fantastic machine,
designed by his own skills and the skills of his parrot.
The small parts composing the machine were just
so many ideas pulled from his mind. Contemplating
all these ideas as they interacted, he thought
he glimpsed the initial idea at their origin,
one clear and distinct idea which contained
in itself all reality and all perfection.

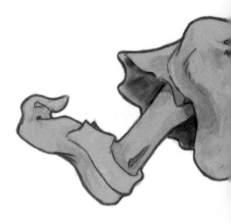

In contemplating the perfection of this idea,
Mister Descartes felt a joy more marvelous
than any he had ever before experienced.
He gave this idea a name: God.

How can I, a finite thing who is neither all-knowing nor all-powerful, have a clear and distinct idea of something infinite?

In what way did this idea of God come to my mind?
For I have never encountered God with my senses,
and yet this idea necessarily comes from something
clearly infinite...

Would God himself have put this idea in my mind
when he created me, like the potter's mark on his clay?

Completely waking up, Mister Descartes examined this idea of the infinite that God himself had placed deeply within all the treasures of his mind.

Let's see then: God is infinite, God is all-powerful, God is perfect in every way. To sum up, God lacks nothing. He therefore can also not be lacking in... existence! In fact, existing is as surely tied to God as the valley is to the mountain, or as three sides are to a triangle... and since God is perfect, he would not want me to be deceived... How could the things of this world then seem so doubtful?

As for Baruch, he was watching with sharp interest a gnat in a very unfortunate position in a spider's web.

Mister Descartes wished to have the experience of being cut off from material things. He burrowed down in his bed, hid under his pillow, and covered his ears, but he found it impossible not to feel his hands pressing against his head, the weight of the covers, and a slight odor of freshly-baked bread wafting up from a merchant's stall under his window.

Even if all these things were but the fruit of his imagination,
Mister Descartes could not completely ignore them.

This is what is so strange:
I, a thinking thing, cannot manage to separate myself
entirely from this body of mine! And it would even seem
as though this smell of fresh bread brings a certain joy
to my mind!

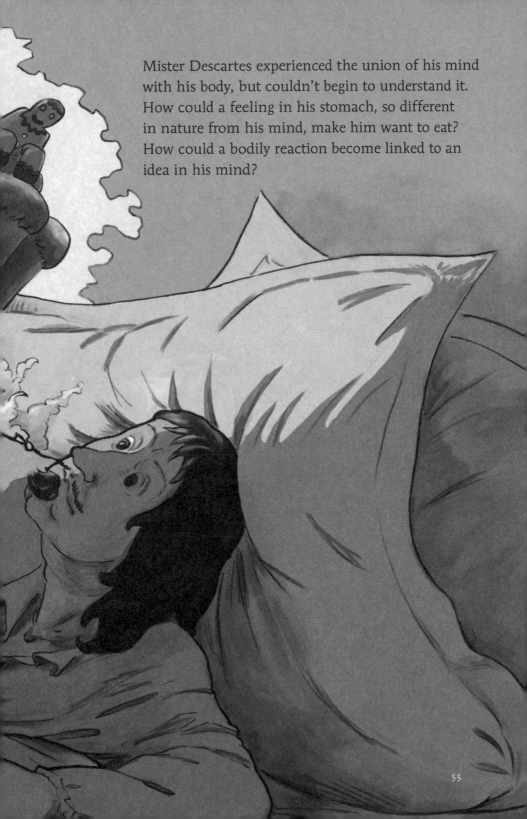

Mister Descartes experienced the union of his mind with his body, but couldn't begin to understand it. How could a feeling in his stomach, so different in nature from his mind, make him want to eat? How could a bodily reaction become linked to an idea in his mind?

Mister Descartes remembered one night of battle
when he had seen soldiers whose arm or leg had been
severed, still feeling pain in their amputated limbs.

"Who knows what the body can do?" asked Baruch

Mister Descartes knew about similar illusions.
While sleeping, the machine in his dream had seemed
as real to him as everything now appeared to be.
Quite obviously, he could not rely upon his senses.

It would be better to think of as separate on the one hand,
this mind that I am and which I can inspect and,
on the other hand, this body in which strange things happen…

As he slid out of bed, he stumbled over Baruch who
was taking a stroll and who replied with a sharp peck
from his beak.

Arrgh!

Mortally struck on his little toe, Mister Descartes confronted
Baruch, who hadn't had his breakfast and wasn't about
to let go of such an easily obtained tidbit. Mister Descartes
understood that he didn't occupy his body like a captain
his ship, but that he was united to and part of this body,
so that when injured on his foot, he had felt pain, unlike
the captain who sees something break in his vessel.
He therefore judged it useful and reasonable to do his best
to shake the pest off his foot.

Studying his nibbled little toe, Mister Descartes realized
that his senses were reliable more often than not.
Moreover, he could use several different senses in order to
examine the same thing, and use his memory to connect
present to past knowledge.

If Baruch appeared and disappeared all of a sudden, as do pictures when I sleep, then he would be a ghost or a phantom created by my mind rather than a real parrot.

But now I know that I am not dreaming. Because my dreams do not correspond to each other as does the whole of my life when I am awake.

Baruch peacefully came and went in front of his master, and Mister Descartes was able to connect this beautiful morning to the rest of his life.

Leaning his ear to the noise of the street, savoring the warmth of the sun, summoning all of his senses, his memory and his understanding, Mister Descartes found not a single thing out of harmony with anything else, and ceased to doubt their truthfulness.

French edition
Jean Paul Mongin & François Schwoebel:
Le Malin Génie de Monsieur Descartes
Design: Yohanna Nguyen
© Les petits Platons, Paris 2012

First edition
ISBN 978-3-03734-546-7
© diaphanes, Zurich-Berlin 2016

www.platoandco.net
www.diaphanes.com

Layout: 2edit, Zurich
Printed and bound in Germany

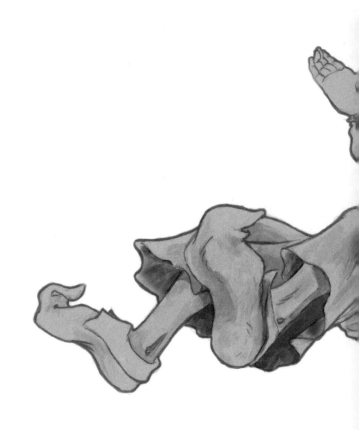